25 WAYS

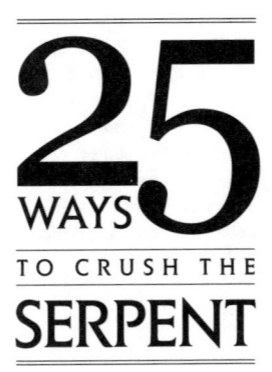

TO CRUSH THE

SERPENT

25 WAYS TO CRUSH THE SERPENT © 2020 TAN Books

All rights reserved. With the exception of short excerpts used in critical review, no part of this work may be reproduced, transmitted, or stored in any form whatsoever, without the prior written permission of the publisher.

This compilation is derived from *The Spiritual Combat*, by Dom. Lorenzo Scupoli. English translation © 1818, W. Pickering and Co., Dublin, and *Sermons from the Latins: Adapted from Bellarmine, Segneri, and other Sources*, Benziger Brothers, New York, 1902, and *The Glories of Mary*, TAN, Charlotte, NC, 2012. Prayers are taken from the *Missale Romanum*, Rome 1920. Quotes from the Saints are taken from public domain sources. Arranged with quotes from Scripture and the saints, and prayers translated from the Extraordinary form of the Mass by Ryan Grant

Unless otherwise noted, the editor's use of the Douay-Rheims Version for Biblical Quotations has been retained. Typography and changes in this edition are the property of TAN Books, and may not be reproduced, in whole or in part, without written permission of the publisher.

Cover & interior design by www.davidferrisdesign.com

Cover Image: Alexvectors © Shutterstock.com
Interior Image: The Virgin Mary Detail of painting. Verona. Italy (photo) Godong / Bridgeman Images

ISBN: 978-15051-1-758-5

Published in the United States by
TAN Books
PO Box 410487
Charlotte, NC 28241
www.TANBooks.com
Printed in the United States of America

25 WAYS

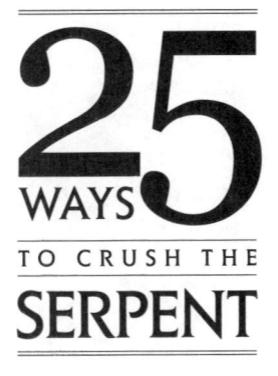

TO CRUSH THE
SERPENT

TAN Books
Charlotte, NC
2020

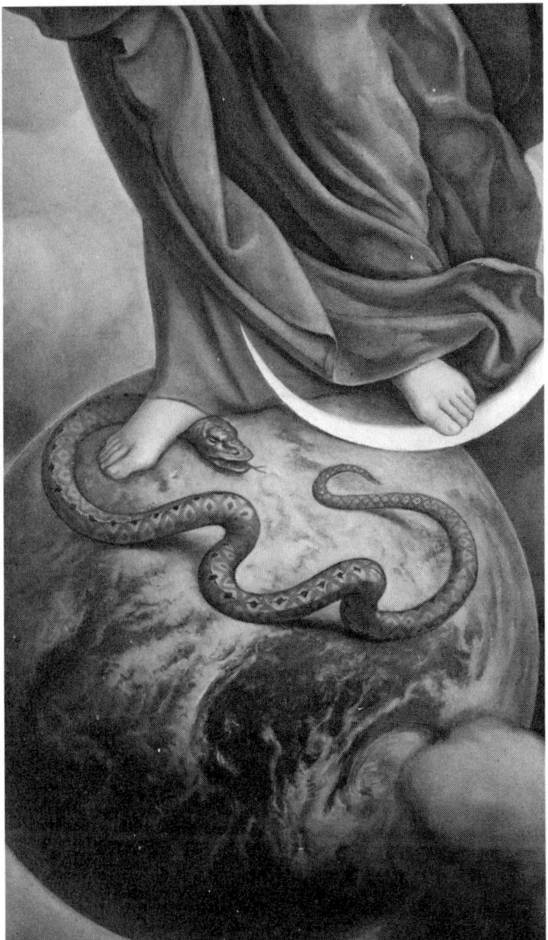

1

FIGHT VALIANTLY AGAINST THE DEVIL

"I saw Satan fall like lightning."

–Luke 10:18

However weak you may be; however formidable your enemies may seem either by their numbers or strength, still be not daunted. The assistance that you have from heaven is more powerful than all that hell can send to destroy the grace of God in your soul. God, who created and redeemed you, is no less than Almighty, and more desirous of your salvation than the devil can be of your destruction.

So, fight valiantly, and do not fail to mortify yourself. For it is by making continual war on your disorderly affections and vicious habits that you will gain the victory, acquire the kingdom of heaven, and unite your soul to God for all eternity.

V. We adore Thee O Christ and we bless Thee;

R. Because by Thy Holy Cross Thou hast redeemed the world.

O Lord, heed our supplications and dispose the path of your servants in the prosperity of your salvation; so that among all the many trials of the road and of this life, they may always be preserved by your help.

2

TRUST IN YOUR GUARDIAN ANGEL

"The angel of God has been my keeper going from here, abiding there, and returning hither."

–Judith 13:20

The devil is always prepared to insight any thought which may lead to our ruin. At the same time, God has appointed to every man on earth his own Guardian Angel. From the first moment of its creation until the settlement of its final destiny, the angel of God is by its side. In joy and sorrow, through virtue and through sin, the faithful monitor is ever there, beseeching, prompting or applauding. From the lost soul he parts reluctant at the gates of hell, or stands triumphant at the heavenly portals to welcome in his charge. It helps us to realize the value of a human soul to think how God has hedged him roundabout with safeguards and protectors. In their hands the angels bear the just man up, lest perhaps he dash his foot against a stone.

Seven times a day the just man falls and he continues just, for the guilt of sin is not so much in the falling as in the staying down.

The guardian angel's concerns in your soul are:
- To awake you from sin;
- To keep you away from all persons, places and things that might cause a relapse;
- To help you persevere;
- To help you put to flight the devils that beset your path, by inspiring prayer and meditations.

Angel of God, my guardian dear,
To whom God's love commits me here;
Ever this day be at my side
To light and guard, to rule and guide.
Amen.

3

FIDELITY TO BAPTISMAL GRACE

"Our glory is this, the testimony of our conscience, that in simplicity of heart and sincerity of God, and not in carnal wisdom, but in the grace of God, we have conversed in this world; and more abundantly towards you."

–2 Corinthians 1:12

All Christians are asked, either by themselves or by their Godparents, whether they renounce the devil, and all his works and pomps. And they answer: ***"I do renounce them."***

But how many renounce them in word and not in reality! On the other hand, how few are there who do not follow the pomps and works of the devil!

Yet, through Baptism, man is brought from a miserable captivity of original sin to a place in the most glorious kingdom! The more this Grace is to be admired, so much the more is man's ingratitude to be detested. Many begin to renounce this wonderful benefit of God, and to enroll themselves the slaves of the devil even before they arrive at the age of reason.

Unless we preserve either our baptismal grace, or by true penance again renounce the devil, return to the service of God, and preserve in it till the end of our life, we cannot possibly live well. Rather, we will be delivered to a miserable death.

But God sees all things, and will not be mocked. He that desires to live well and to die well, let him enter into the chamber of his heart, and not deceive himself. Let him seriously and attentively consider over and over again whether he is in love with the pomps of this world, or with sins, which are the works of the devil; and whether he gives them a place in his heart, his words, and actions.

> *Let us pray.*
> O God, who resists the proud and gives grace to the humble, grant unto us the virtue of true humility, the form of which Your only begotten Son showed to the faithful, so that being lifted up we might never provoke your indignation, but rather more, being lowered, we might take up the gifts of Your grace. Through the same Christ our Lord, Amen

4

PRESERVE YOUR PEACE OF SOUL

"Now the Lord of Peace himself gives you everlasting peace in every place."

–2 Thessalonians 3:16

Preserving a peaceful mind in all occurrences of life, your advantage will be very great; but without it, your pious exercises will come to nothing. The devil is ever solicitous to banish peace from your mind, knowing well that God only dwells there in peace, and that it is in peace that he works his wonders. Hence, it is that Satan employs all his cunning to destroy it; foments anxiety to the insults of your enemy, causes confusion when discerning the sure and ready path to virtue. In order to surprise us, he does not hesitate to inspire seemingly good designs, but once undertaken, are otherwise in effect, as is easily discovered by their disturbing our inward peace.

To remedy so dangerous an evil, when the enemy endeavors to put us upon some new design, let us beware of giving it entrance too hastily into our hearts. First let us renounce all affection arising from self-love; then offer the design to God, begging with great earnestness, that He will manifest to us whether it comes from Him, or our enemy. Finally consult your good pastor or a faithful mentor before you begin.

> Give peace, O Lord, in our days; for there is none other that fighteth for us, but only Thou, our God.

> V. Let there be peace in thy strength, O Lord.

> R. And plenty in thy strong places.

> *Let us pray.*
> O God, from whom proceed all holy desires, all right counsels and just works; grant unto us thy servants that peace which the world cannot give, that our hearts may be devoted to thy service, and that, being delivered from the fear of our enemies, we may pass our time in peace under thy protection. Through Christ our Lord. Amen.

5

DO NOT BE ANXIOUS

*"Do not be anxious for tomorrow,
for the morrow will be anxious for itself."*

–Matthew 5:34

Anxiety happens to fearful souls, who are in continual dread of the enemy. Ever apprehensive of having more laid upon them than they can bear, or suffer. Know then, that in anxiety there lurks a poison which not only infects the first seeds of virtues, but even destroys those that are already formed.

What the worm does in wood, anxiety does to the spiritual life. It has been employed too successfully by the devil to draw men into his snares, especially those that aspire to perfection.

Watch over yourself, and be attached to prayer and good works. Do not defer making your nuptial robe until you are called upon to go forth and meet the heavenly bridegroom.

To dispel anxiety, spend at least 30 minutes before the Blessed Sacrament, either in Adoration or simply in a Church where it is reserved, and conclude with the following prayer:

> We ask You, O Lord, shatter the pride of our enemies, and lay low their contumacy by the power of your right hand. Through the same Christ our Lord, Amen.
>
> "Let nothing disturb you, nothing frighten you, all things are passing,
> God is unchanging. Patience gains all; nothing is lacking to those who have God: God alone is sufficient."
>
> – **St. Teresa of Avila**

6

BELIEVE YOU CAN BE FORGIVEN

"Behold, I am the Lord, the God of all flesh; shall anything be hard for me?"

–Jeremiah 32:27

When you feel wounded, that is to have fallen into any sin, whether through weakness or deliberately through malice, do not be overly downcast. Do not abandon yourself to grief, rather, trust in God with great but humble confidence, and excite a lively sorrow for your fault. Then with calmness, show your displeasure against those passions which reign most in your heart, especially that which occasioned your fall. Say, "Lord, what might I not have done, had not your infinite goodness come to my assistance?

After confessing your sins, do not be troubled over whether God has pardoned you or not. This is a needless trouble and a loss of time, proceeding only from pride, and the illusion of the devil, who under specious pretexts, seeks to disturb you. Instead, abandon yourself to the divine mercy, and pursue your usual exercises with as much tranquility as if you had not committed any fault. Though you should fall several times in a day, yet lose not a just confidence in Him.

> Lord have mercy,
> Christ have mercy,
> Lord have mercy.

> *Let us pray.*
> O Lord Jesus Christ, who came down from heaven, from the bosom of the Father, to earth, and poured forth Your precious blood in remission for our sins, we humbly ask you, that on the day of judgment we might merit to hear, while standing at your right hand: "Come you blessed men!" Who lives and reigns with God the Father and the Holy Spirit, God for ever and ever. Amen.

7

DO NOT DESPAIR

"Do not think the burning heat which is to try you is something strange, as if some new thing happened to you; if you partake of the sufferings of Christ, rejoice, that when His glory shall be revealed, you may also be glad with joy."

– **1 Peter 4:13**

The enemy throws on our path a vain terror that causes us to despair over the sight of our past sins. If you perceive yourself in any danger of this kind, take it as a general rule that the remembrance of former crimes comes from divine grace and is salutary if it forms in you sentiments of humility, sorrow and confidence in God's mercy. If, on the other hand, it causes disturbance and despondency, and leaves you spiritless and daunted, believing you are beyond hope then it is the devil.

In such circumstances, do nothing but humble yourself, and place a greater confidence than ever in the boundless mercy of God. Although you should be truly sorry for having offended such sovereign goodness whenever you call to mind your past sins, still you should ask pardon with a firm confidence in the merits of our Savior. This will defeat the devil's plan, as it turns his own weapons against him, and gives greater glory to God.

> Ah, my Jesus! Remind me always of the death you suffered for me, and give me confidence. I tremble lest the devil should make me despair at death by bringing before my view the many acts of treason I have committed against You. How many promises have I made never more to offend You. How many promises have I made never more to offend You after the light You have given me! And after these promises, I have, with the hope of pardon, again turned my back upon You. Then, have I insulted You because You did not chastise me? My redeemer! Give me a great sorrow for my sins before I leave this world. Mary, my Mother! Obtain for me these graces, along with holy perseverance till death.
>
> – St. Alphonsus Liguori

8

CONCUPISCENCE IS CONQUERED BY PRAYER

"O God! How many souls does this sin drag down to Hell!"

–St. John Vianney

Do not presume on your own strength. This is so even if after many years spent in the world, you have been proof against the force of concupiscence. For the devil of lust often achieves in one instant, what whole years could not effect. Sometimes he is very long in preparing for the assault, but then the blow is all the more severe, and the wound the more dangerous, for being dissembled, and coming when least expected.

The danger is always greatest – where there is the least appearance of evil. Impure inclinations imperceptibly insinuate themselves into seemingly innocent friendships by frequent visits, flirtations and indiscreet familiarities. The poison reaches the heart, and reason is blinded and violent and almost irresistible temptations arise.

Instead:
- Flee all occasions of sin, which you are more susceptible to than straw is to fire;
- Do not rely on your own virtue, or a resolution, or strength since no matter how well disposed you may be to virtue, temptation will kindle a fire that is hard to extinguish
- Pray 3 Hail Marys upon rising every single day.

When your passions rebel, rebel against them.
When they fight, fight them.
When they attack you, you attack them.
Only beware lest they conquer you.

–**St. Augustine**

9

DO NOT BE DISTRACTED BY PAST SINS

"Be angry and do not sin: the things you say in your hearts, be sorry for them upon your beds."

–Psalm 4:5

The devil lays many snares for those walking on the narrow road of the spiritual life. It is important to condemn a certain interior regret, which though seemingly coming from God, as being a remorse of conscience for past faults, yet is doubtless the work of the devil. If such an interior regret tends to our greater humiliation, if it increases our fervor in performing good works and our confidence in the Divine Mercy, we ought to receive it with great thankfulness as a gift from heaven. But if such regrets occasion anxiety; or renders us dispirited, slothful, timorous and backward in our duty, we may certainly conclude, that it proceeds from the enemy, and ought to be passed over without the least regard.

Rest in the provident care of God's holy Mother:
We fly to thy patronage,
O holy Mother of God;
despise not our petitions in our necessities,
but deliver us always from all dangers,
O glorious and blessed Virgin.
Amen.

10

DO NOT PERSIST IN SIN

"To sin is human, but to persist in sin is devilish."
–St. Catherine of Siena

When the devil entangles a soul into sin, all his plans are made ready to distract it from the horrible state that it is in. Not content with stifling all inspirations that come from heaven, he endeavors to plunge the soul further by furnishing dangerous opportunities into fresh crimes, either of the same or a more enormous nature. Hence it is, that deprived of the light of heaven, the soul heaps sins upon sins, and hardens itself in iniquity. Thus, it wallows in the mire, and rushes from darkness to darkness, flying farther than ever from the path of salvation.

The most efficacious remedy against this evil, is to receive without the least resistance the divine inspirations, which will recall the soul from darkness to light, from vice to virtue, repeating prayers with great fervor, "Lord, help me!" Go immediately into confession, and if this is not possible, make an act of perfect contrition every day until you are able to go. Make a firm resolution not to sin again.

AN ACT OF CONTRITION
O my God, I am truly sorry for having offended You, Whom I should love above all things. It is this offense against your divine majesty, more than the fear of hell, which brings contrition for my sins. I firmly intend, with the help of your grace, to go to Confession, to do penance, to sin no more and to avoid all the near occasions of sin. Amen.

I would give my life a thousand times that God might not be offended.

–**St. Gerard Majella**

11

DO NOT WAIT TO GO TO CONFESSION

"The night is passed, and the day is at hand. Let us, therefore, cast off the works of darkness, and put on the armor of light."

–**Romans 13:12**

Those who wish to turn away from a life of sin are often deluded by the devil, who tries to persuade them that they have a long time to live. Consequently, they think that they may safely delay in confessing. He suggests to them that this or that business must first be settled before they can take the steps of going to confession.

Others are ready, here and now, to confess their sins, but then they think of the person of the priest, and because they are known to him, they fear to confess out of human respect, and so delay their confession until another priest may be available. They may do this even if this takes several weeks or may require travel, lest they think they may lose the good opinion of the priest, as if he has not heard all of these things before.

These snares have, and daily do, entangle many. But they have no one to blame but themselves, since in this matter only the glory of God and their own salvation should be considered. Do not say, tomorrow, but rather, now!

> If my conscience were burdened with all the sins it is possible to commit, I would still go and throw myself into our Lord's arms, my heart all broken up with contrition. I know what tenderness He has for any prodigal child of His that comes back to Him.
>
> **– St Thérèse of Lisieux**

12

AVOID MORTAL SIN

Can any sin be called light, since every sin involves some contempt of God?

–St Eucherius

Many people think that stopping mortal sin is the final goal of the spiritual life. But it is just a beginning–and how necessary! By mortal sin we justly fall under the slavery of the devil, but not irredeemably. It is never too late to appeal to divine mercy to have patience. The case is never so hopeless that, relying on the infinite merits of Our Redeemer, we can confidently promise God's justice to pay Him all. One thing, and one only, is necessary; that, as we fell by pride so we rise by humbly falling, as supplicants, at God's feet, for: "He that exalts himself shall be humbled, and he that humbles himself shall be exalted."

Let us pray:
Almighty and kind God, who produced a fountain of living water from a rock for Your thirsty people, draw out tears of compunction from the hardness of our heart, so that we might avail to mourn for our sins, as well as merit to receive remission for them from your mercy. Through the same Christ our Lord. Amen.

13

AVOID THE NEAR OCCASIONS OF SIN

"He that looks at a woman lustfully, has already committed adultery in his heart."

–Matthew 5:28

The powers of resistance desert the gambler in the gaming house, the drunkard in the bar, and the lustful at the sight of immodesty. How wickedly wise the devil is! When he tempted Christ he did not show on a map all the kingdoms of the world that he promised Him, but took Him up into a high mountain and showed them to Him, hoping that an actual view of them and the glory thereof would cause the Savior to fall down and worship him. How rash, then, and presumptuous it is for you that have but lately fled from sin to knowingly tread again the dark and crooked alleyways of vice, where every doorway hides the occasion where the devil will restore you to sin. It is unhappily true that in an instant one can pass from virtue to vice, but the opposite is not so! We do not pass from vice to virtue instantly. When God forbids a thing, he also forbids its near occasions.

- Our first parents were forbidden not only to eat the fruit, but even to touch it.
- The Israelites were forbidden not only to adore idols, but even to possess them.
- Christ too, when reaffirming the commandments, not only forbade the sinful deed but the longing glance, the interior passion, the foul thought, the covetous desire.
- Is technology an occasion for us to sin? Do we throw away our time on social media? Does doing so become an occasion for us to calumniate our neighbor? To view vain and useless "news"? To see immodesty which can lead to the vice of lust? If it is not necessary, we should remove it altogether.

Almighty and Eternal God, deepen our faith, our hope and our charity, so that we may attain what You have promised and love what You have commanded. Through Christ our Lord, Amen.

14

DO NOT FEAR THE DEVIL

"The names of Jesus and Mary have special power to banish the temptations of the devil."

–St. Alphonsus Liguori

St. Francis was once so consumed in prayer in the Portiuncula, that the devil found his kingdom to be in ruins. Angry, he sent to devils to assault the saint and disturb his prayer. St. Francis paid them no heed, and the devils lifted him out of the chapel and began to afflict him with severe physical blows. Even then, the saint laughed, declaring that if God gave them the power to kill him, then glory unto Him; but if not, they could not hurt him at all. Thus, the devils suffered more in delivering blows than St. Francis did in receiving them.

In like manner, we have been given the spirit of freedom through our baptism, not to walk constantly in fear of this or that demonic assault, but to have the spirit of freedom of the sons of God. Thus, when disturbed by any demonic assault, we should make prayers of deliverance, not in the spirit of fear, but in the spirit of confidence and trust in God.

> St. Michael the Archangel, defend us in battle. Be our defense against the wickedness and snares of the Devil.
> May God rebuke him, we humbly pray, and do thou, O Prince of the heavenly hosts, by the power of God, thrust into hell Satan, and all the evil spirits, who prowl about the world seeking the ruin of souls. Amen.

15

FEAR THE TORMENTS OF HELL

"It is better to enter lame into eternal life than having two feet, to be cast into the hell of unquenchable fire, where the worm does not die, and the fire is not extinguished."

–Mark 9:44-45

Unhappy sinners who are lulled to rest by the illusions of the world, and who live as if there were no hell will be suddenly stripped of their illusions by the most frightful of catastrophes. From the midst of their pleasures they shall fall into the Pit of Torments. Then, what a surprise! What a sudden change! But what will it be when the sinner shall see himself, in the twinkling of an eye, in the pit of hell?

Yet, the fear of hell must properly be balanced with a love of God. Fear of hell is not enough to get us to heaven. God does not seek service rendered out of fear, but loving service. Our fallen nature being what it is, we also need a further stimulus when, during temptation and confusion, the love of God is blurred. With the fear of hell, we properly see the devil and the false happiness which he offers us in this world for what it truly is, by seeing what it leads to.

When tempted:
- Think upon the terrible suffering that sinners must endure in hell;
- Think of the joys of heaven and how terrible their loss would be;
- Make an act of contrition frequently, to make habitual the true sorrow for sins, and provide against sudden death;
- Have confidence and love of God in all things.

If I saw the gates of Hell open and I stood on the brink of the abyss, I should not despair, I should not lose hope of mercy, because I should trust in Thee, my God.

–St Gemma Galgani

16

KNOW YOURSELF TO CRUSH THE SERPENT

"The fear of the Lord is the beginning of wisdom. Fools despise wisdom and instruction."

–Proverbs 1:7

When the devil is defeated once or twice, he will not fail to renew the attack yet a third time. He tries to make us forget the vices and passions we actually labor under, and fills our imagination with vain projects of an ideal perfection, to which he knows we shall never reach. By this contrivance we receive frequent and dangerous wounds, without ever thinking of how to remedy them. These imaginary desires pass to real effects, and through a secret pride we value ourselves as great saints. In this way, when we cannot tolerate the least difficulty, we amuse ourselves with imagining we are ready to suffer the greatest torments, even the pains of purgatory, for the love of God. Really, what we feel, affected with sufferings at a distance, compares itself with those who actually bear the greatest pains.

To avoid this trap, we must resolve to fight, and actually engage where we are. Then we will see whether our resolutions are cowardly or courageous, and so advance to perfection through the road the saints have marked out.

> Dear Lord, you know my weakness. Each morning I resolve to be humble, and in the evening I recognize that I have often been guilty of pride. The sight of these faults tempts me to discouragement. Yet I know that discouragement itself is a form of pride. I wish, therefore, O my God, to build all my trust upon You. As You can do all things, deign to implant in my soul this virtue which I desire. And to obtain it from Thy Infinite Mercy, I will often say to Thee: "Jesus, meek and humble of Heart, make my heart like unto Thine."
>
> –St. Therese of Lisieux

17

REMOVE YOUR PRINCIPAL FAULT
(BEFORE IT IS TOO LATE)

"He that shall persevere unto the end, he shall be saved."

–Matthew 10:22

If you only mind God when it is suitable for you, little wonder then if at your death God will fail to grant you a morsel of repentance, however much you desire it. But God's mercy, you will say! True, but the measure of grace He will accord you, though enough to sanctify the average man, will not suffice to save a soul with such a past as yours. Your ruling passion, be it drink, or lust, or hate, or whatever, will be strong in death, because at death, since it is the crisis in the battle between the powers of light and darkness, the devil, like a skillful general, will marshal all his forces for the final struggle.

- St. Vincent Ferrer believed deathbed conversions were more miraculous than raising the dead;
- The habits toward vice you form in life will be moving you to sin at your death;
- Final impenitence is not to be taken lightly; always work to make a good act of Contrition and to strive to break the attachment to sin.

Almighty and merciful God, who conferred the remedies of salvation and the gifts of eternal life upon the human race, look mercifully upon your servants, and revive the souls which you created, so that in the hour of their departure, they might merit to be displayed to their creator through the hands of the holy angels without the stain of sin. Through the same Christ our Lord. Amen.

18

AVOID HIDDEN PRIDE

"If anyone thinks he is something, whereas he is nothing, he deceives himself."

–**Galatians 6:3**

The devil will even tempt us by virtue itself. He inspires us with esteem and complacency for ourselves, and lifts us up to that pitch that we cannot escape the snares of vain-glory. So, fortify yourself with the knowledge of your own nothingness, and be ever mindful that of yourself you are nothing and can do nothing. Remember that you are full of sin and deserve nothing but perdition, were it not for the graces given to us by our Savior. Let this important truth be always before you, and if any thoughts of vanity and presumption arise, repel them as the most dangerous enemies who have vowed your destruction.

Use the following method:
- Carefully distinguish in your actions between what is your own and what is due to God and His grace;
- Consider this life, which you only hold through God's infinite mercy, and what you would be without Him;
- Would you not return every instant to what his omnipotence drew you from, unless continually preserved by him?
- Even if you were in a state of grace, without the assistance of heaven, where would be your merit? What good could you perform?

O Jesus, meek and humble of heart,
Make my heart like unto Thine.

19

GROW IN DEVOTION TO MARY

"I will put enmities between you and the woman, and your seed and her seed; she shall crush your head, and you shall lie in wait for her heel."

–**Gen. 3:15.**

Not only is the most Blessed Virgin queen of heaven and of all the saints, but she also overcame hell and all evil spirits by her virtues. St. John Damascene saluted the Blessed Virgin and called her "hope of those who are in despair." St. Ephrem calls her "the safe harbor of all sailing on the sea of this world." St. Bonaventure exhorts even the desperate not to despair, and full of joy and tenderness towards this most dear mother, he lovingly exclaimed: "And who, O Lady, can be without confidence in you, since you assist even those who are in despair? I do not doubt that whenever we have recourse to you, we shall obtain what we desire. So, let any man who is without hope, hope in you." We cannot fail to call upon Mary, the Immaculate Mother of Christ, in all trials, especially when we are engaged in battle with the devil.

The infernal spirits tremble at the very thought of Mary, and of her august name! The devils tremble even if they only hear the name of Mary. Just as men fall prostrate with fear if a thunderbolt falls near them, so do the devils if they hear the name of Mary.

To defeat the devil with Mary's help:
- Cultivate daily devotion to the Blessed Virgin;
- Call upon her mighty aid in temptation and trial;
- Do not suffer your mind to be afflicted or disturbed, but call upon the name of Mary.

MEMORARE
Remember, O most gracious Virgin Mary, that never was it known that anyone who fled to thy protection, implored thy help, or sought thine intercession was left unaided. Inspired by this confidence, I fly unto thee, O Virgin of virgins, my mother; to thee do I come, before thee I stand, sinful and sorrowful. O Mother of the Word Incarnate, despise not my petitions, but in thy mercy hear and answer me. Amen.

20

AVOID DELUSIONS OF GRANDEUR

"Do not think you are wiser than you are, but be wise in sobriety, and according as God has divided to everyone the measure of faith."

–**Romans 12:3**

If the devil perceives that we are on the path towards heaven, and that we desire God alone, he transforms himself into an angel of light. He urges us to attain perfection, hurrying us on blindly and without the least regard to our weakness; he fills our heads with devout thoughts, and even examples from Scripture and the saints, to draw us into some shameful false step, through an indiscreet and precipitate fervor. He will spur us on to excessive fasting, disciplines, taking on vast amounts of prayer, and like things. He purposes us to have a notion of performing wonders when really, we fall prey to vanity, become dispirited with works that exceed our strength, grow tired of the devout life, and return to the vanities of the world.

Consider that:
- While many are not capable of imitating the austerities of the saints, everyone may imitate them in specific virtues;
- They may imitate the saints in their contempt of the world and themselves;
- They may imitate the saints in their humility and charity to all men;
- In returning good for evil to their worst enemies;
- Avoid even the smallest faults, which are more meritorious in the sight of God than all corporal severities.

O God, who sees that we are destitute of all virtue, guard us inwardly and outwardly, so that we might be fortified from all adversity in body, and cleansed in mind from wicked thoughts. Through the same Christ our Lord, Amen.

21

AVOID RASH JUDGMENT

"The love of our neighbor works no evil. Love, therefore, is the fulfilling of the law."

–Romans 13:10

We not only encourage rash judgment in our own heart, but try to spread it to others. This vice is nourished by pride, and the more we give way to it, the more conceited we become in ourselves, and the more exposed we are to the devil's delusions. The devil no sooner discovers this malicious propensity in us, than he immediately employs all his skill to make us attentive to the failings of others, and to magnify them beyond the truth.

As the devil is vigilant in pointing out the faults of our neighbor, let us be at least as vigilant in discovering and defeating his designs. When he suggests to us the sins of others:

- Let us banish all such thoughts;
- Let us have an abhorrence of malicious insinuations;

- Let us remember that we are not to judge the souls of others;
- Blinded with prejudice and passion, we are naturally inclined to put the worst interpretation on our neighbor's actions; let us remember instead to presume the best interpretation;
- Let us remember our own wretchedness, where we shall find so much room for amendment, as to have little inclination to judge and condemn others.

O God, by whom desires are made holy, counsels right and works just, grant to Your servants that peace which the world cannot give, so that both our hearts may be dedicated to your commands, and that our days may be peaceful with your protection. Through the Same Christ our Lord, Amen.

22

OVERCOME SPIRITUAL DRYNESS

"He had turned aside, and was gone. My soul melted when he spoke; I sought him, and found him not; I called, and he did not answer me."

–Song of Songs 5:6

Spiritual dryness is a necessary step on the spiritual life, infused into our souls by the Holy Spirit so as to wean us from everything which is not of God. But most who assume they have it in fact do not, but rather, have only begun cutting away unhealthy attachments to the world. When spiritual dryness takes root in worldly people, it is almost certainly from the devil, who sets all engines at work to make us negligent, to lead us out of the way of perfection, and plunge us again into the vanities of the world.

When you find yourself suffering spiritual distaste and dryness, look to whether it is owing to any fault of your own, and amend it at once; not so much with a view of regaining the sweetness which has been changed to bitterness, but to banish everything that is in the least displeasing to God, and to dispel any occasion for the cunning serpent to work upon the soul.

> O God, Who made all things benefit those who love you, grant to our hearts the inviolable affect of your charity, so that the desires, conceived from your inspiration, cannot be changed into any temptation. Through the same Christ our Lord. Amen.

23

PREPARE FOR TRIALS OF FAITH

"But though we, or an angel from heaven, preach a gospel to you besides that which we have preached to you, let him be anathema."

–Galatians 1:8

If the enemy offers a captivating and fallacious argument, do not enter into any dispute with him. Let it be enough to say with indignation, "begone Satan, father of lies! I believe only what the Holy Catholic Church believes."

In the same way, be on your guard against any thoughts which offer themselves as strengthening your faith. Reject these too as suggestions of the devil, who seeks to disturb you, by insensibly engaging you in a dispute. But if you cannot free yourself from such thoughts, and your head is full of them, still, be strong and do not listen to the devil's argument, or even passages of scripture that he may bring to your notice. No matter how clear and direct they may seem, he will certainly quote them wrong.

If someone asks you what the Church believes with a mind to wrangle over some ambiguous word, content yourself with making one general act of faith, or if you desire to mortify the devil still more, respond that the Church believes the truth.

> O God, do not despise Your people, who cry out to You in affliction, but, on account of the glory of Your Name, be pleased to come to the assistance of those in tribulation. Through Christ our Lord, Amen.

24

DO NOT GIVE UP

> *"Be faithful until death, and I will give you the crown of life."*
>
> **–Apocalypse 2:10**

Whenever we are engaged in a work of piety, prayer, or anything else, we will experience a certain level of dryness. Sometimes we are distracted by worldly things, and have a powerful desire to stop our prayer, and then do not come back to it! Never quit any work of piety, no matter how little relish you might find in it, unless you would comply with what the devil desires. Keep at it, and you will discover the great advantages to be gained through a humble perseverance in works of piety, when attended with the most irksome spiritual barrenness. It is only through humility and patience that we may reap the benefit of such work.

To unmask the serpent in these trials:
- When preparing for any work of piety, if some business arises to distract you, put it off and make your prayer first;
- If you begin to pray, but find a burning desire to check social media, banish the thought and focus on prayer;
- Do not go hasty to pious works. Prepare yourself for at least a few minutes before by reading Scripture, lives of the saints, or good spiritual material. If you attempt to pray immediately after engaging in worldly things, you will find yourself continually distracted.

O God, who justifies the impious and does not will the death of the sinner, we humbly beg your majesty, that you would mercifully preserve your servants trusting in your mercy with assistance that they may continually serve you and never be separated from you by any temptations. Through Christ our Lord, Amen.

25

GOD IS VICTORIOUS OVER THE DEVIL

"Now is come salvation, and strength, and the kingdom of our God, and the power of his Christ: because the accuser of our brethren is cast forth, who accused them before our God day and night."

–Apocalypse 12:10

In the beginning, man's animal passions were as a mighty fire that had just begun and raged fiercely, but God subdued them by the waters of the Deluge and tempered them still more since by the waters of Baptism. The Devil's powers too, have been curtailed since the woman Mary crushed the serpent's head, and her divine Son placed at our disposal the means of repelling him. The way to heaven has been made very smooth by the feet of innumerable saints, and easily traced, deeply dyed as it is with the blood of Christ and the martyrs. Moreover, the end has been shown so clear to our view, that the wonder is how, how we can possibly stray from that

More TAN Booklets:

25 Ways to Become a Saint
Wonders of the Holy Name
Queen of Heaven: Prayers for the Battle
Favorite Prayers to St. Joseph
Confession It's Fruitful Practice
Uniformity With God's Will

Visit www.TANBooks.com
Quantity Discounts Available

path, how can we have a single thought but for God and the soul?

> *Make Frequent trips to the Blessed Sacrament:* Visits to the Blessed Sacrament are powerful and indispensable means of overcoming the attacks of the devil. Make frequent visits to Jesus in the Blessed Sacrament and the devil will be powerless against you.
>
> – St John Bosco

We beseech you O Lord, defend us from all dangers of mind and body, and with the blessed and glorious intercession of Mary, the ever-virgin Mother of God, with St. Joseph, your Apostles Peter and Paul and all the saints, mercifully grant us salvation and peace. Amen.